THE GO-KART TRACK

written by Jeremy Strong
illustrated by Ken Stott

Chapter One

A Champion

The finishing line for the marathon race was on the High Street. Hundreds of people lined the street, waiting to see who was going to win. Ben and Tessa and their dad, Josh, were there. Anna King was running in the women's race.

"There they are!" cried Ben, as the runners came into view. They were still some way from the finish. "I can't see Mum."

As the runners got closer, the Kings could see the bunch of front runners more clearly.

"I still can't see Mum," said Tessa. "Where is she?"

They were all hoping that Anna would be near the front. She was a strong runner and she had been training hard for the marathon.

Josh King held his breath.

He crossed his fingers.

Just then one of the runners broke away from the main bunch and began to sprint for the finish.

"It's Anna!" yelled Mr King. "Go on Anna! You can do it!"

Now the other runners were sprinting too. They were catching up. The children screamed at her. "Run, run! Run your legs off, Mum!"

Anna put on another spurt of speed. She flashed past them. A huge cheer went up from the crowd. Anna King had won!

Anna had to stand on a platform.
She was Number One! She was given
a big silver cup, and an envelope.
She looked very proud.

CONGRATULATIONS

This certificate entitles you and your family to one free visit to

BIFF'S GO-KART TRACK.

When they got home Anna put her feet up, while Josh made tea. Tessa admired the silver cup she had won. Ben asked his mother what was in the envelope.

"I don't know. Let's have a look," she said.

Anna opened the envelope and pulled out a letter with something pinned to it. "Well I never! I've won a prize for the whole family. We've won a day's visit to the new go-kart track. You know, the one they've built near the hospital? We're going go-karting, and it's all free!"

"Wow!" said Josh. "Go-karting. Brrrm! Brrrm! I've always wanted to go racing."

"So have I!" shouted Ben.

"I haven't," scowled Tessa. "Go-karting is stupid. All you do is sit in a little toy car."

"I expect you'll enjoy it when you get there," suggested Mum. Tessa just scowled even more. Ben was bubbling with excitement. "I'm going to beat the lot of you! I'll be the champion."

"Oh no you won't,"
Josh King shook his head.
"I'll be the fastest."

Anna King stared at them both. "Excuse me," she said. "I shall be the fastest on this planet. After all, I've already won the marathon."

All three of them laughed and they looked at Tessa. She folded her arms across her chest. She wouldn't say another word.

Chapter Two

At the Track

They could hear the buzz of the go-karts as soon as they parked their car. When they got to the side of the track they could see the little machines whizzing round.

"They're like bees on wheels!" said Ben.

"ZZZOOM!"

Anna King showed her free tickets.

"So, you won the marathon?" said Biff Morgan. He was the owner of the track. "Well done! Have any of you been in a go-kart before?"

"Only Josh's car," said Anna. "He always drives as if he's in a go-kart."

"No I don't!" Josh complained.

"Yes you do, Dad," nodded Ben, and he grinned at Biff.

"Well, it's all pretty simple," Biff said. "You've got a steering wheel. You know what that's for!"

They nodded, all except for Tessa. She put up her hand. "Excuse me," she said in a silly, baby voice. "What is the steering wheel for?"

Anna nudged Tessa hard. "Tessa!" she hissed. "Stop playing up!"

"Don't worry," laughed Biff. "I like a joke myself. Now, you see these two foot pedals? The one on the left is the brake. The one on the right makes the kart go faster. Got that? Okay, we'll go and get kitted out."

At that moment one of the karts came sliding round a bend much too fast. It crashed into a wall of tyres. The driver got out and shook his head sadly.

"Oh dear," muttered Josh.

"That's my son," laughed Biff. "He's always driving too fast and crashing into things."

"It looks a bit dangerous," said Anna.

"That's why the walls are made of tyres," said Biff. "They absorb the impact."

"It looks brilliant!" Ben shouted. Tessa had gone rather quiet.

Biff took them across to the kit room. There were racing overalls, in all sizes and colours, hanging on the walls. There were shelves full of crash helmets.

It did not take long for them to find the right-sized kit and get changed. Then they stood around staring at each other.

"This is great!" said Ben, pulling on a pair of leather racing gloves.

Anna and Josh knocked their helmets together.

"I always thought you had a hard head," said Josh.

Biff checked their equipment and then they marched down to the pit lane where all the karts were kept. It was time to get out on the track.

Chapter Three

Ready to Race

Ben wanted to go fast straight away, but it was more difficult than he thought. He had to remember what to do with his feet, and watch where he was going, and steer – all at the same time.

They went round the track quite slowly to start with. Biff watched and yelled helpful things at them. “Start turning the wheel just before you get to a corner. As you come out of the corner you can put your right foot down and speed up.”

The first time Ben tried to do this he didn't go round the corner. Instead he went right into it, and the go-kart plunged into the wall of tyres.

"Are you okay?" yelled Josh as he went past.

"I'm fine!" Ben got the kart going again and set off after the others.

After a few laps they all began to speed up. Faster and faster they went. Soon they were buzzing round as quickly as everyone else.

Biff waved a flag and stopped them. "What do you think of it so far?" he asked.

"Fantastic!" chorused three of the Kings.

Tessa just shrugged her shoulders.

"I think it's time the four of you had a race against each other," said Biff.

The four karts lined up alongside each other. Biff stood to one side. He was holding a big klaxon. “This is a ten lap race. Are you ready?” Ben gripped the steering wheel. Anna and Josh nodded. Tessa looked grim. The klaxon blared.

Chapter Four

Two Champions!

With a roar of engines and back tyres skidding, the four go-karts raced towards the first corner. Josh was already in front. His kart snaked round the corner. Ben set off after his father. Anna was coming up alongside. Tessa was last.

Faster and faster they went. Ben could feel the wind whistling past his face. His kart went into a skid, but he managed to get back straight again. Tessa was closing in on Anna. Josh was still in front, getting further and further ahead.

Josh was driving like a champion. He went racing ahead. And then he went just a tiny bit too fast. The kart went into a gigantic skid. Round and round it spun until ...

The kart slid into the tyre wall.

Ben overtook his dad.

Then Anna overtook him.

Then Tessa overtook him too.
Josh grinned and got his kart going again.

Now Tessa was overtaking her mother.

"You can't do that!" yelled Anna, but Tessa was already past her.

Now it was a race between Ben and Tessa. Ben was leading, but not by much. Tessa tucked in behind him. She stayed there, right on his tail. They came to the last corner. The winning flag was in sight. Suddenly Tessa swung out from behind Ben and went zooming past. She had won the race!

Biff said that they had all done very well. "Did you enjoy it?" he asked.

Josh and Ben looked glum. "It was all right," they muttered.

"I prefer marathon running," Anna said. "Tessa can't overtake me then."

"It was fantastic!" yelled Tessa, beaming from ear to ear.

Biff presented her with a prize –
a giant bar of chocolate.

On the way home Tessa and Anna sat in the car, singing happily.

Ben didn't mind. He was looking after the chocolate.